Artificial Intelligence and Anthropomorphism. Does Alan Turings Imitation Game Enhance Anthropomorphism in AI Research?

Tim Mauch

Bibliographic information published by the German National Library:

The German National Library lists this publication in the National Bibliography; detailed bibliographic data are available on the Internet at http://dnb.dnb.de.

ISBN: 9783346392992
This book is also available as an ebook.

© GRIN Publishing GmbH
Nymphenburger Straße 86
80636 München

Print and binding: Books on Demand GmbH, Norderstedt, Germany
Printed on acid-free paper from responsible sources.

The present work has been carefully prepared. Nevertheless, authors and publishers do not incur liability for the correctness of information, notes, links and advice as well as any printing errors.

GRIN web shop: https://www.grin.com/document/1006412

AUGUST 14, 2020

Leuphana Universität Lüneburg
Module: Datafied Humanity

ANTHROPOMORPHISM IN ARTIFICIAL INTELLIGENCE

DOES ALAN TURING'S IMITATION GAME ENHANCE THE ANTHROPO-MORPHISM IN ARTIFICIAL INTELLIGENCE RESEARCH?

TIM MAUCH

Contents

1 Introduction

Artificial intelligence (AI) is one of the newest scientific fields, starting in the middle of the 20th century with the goal of creating intelligent entities (Russel & Norvig, 2010). Nonetheless the scientific roots of the field reach far behind since the history of human-kind – of homo sapiens – has always been coined by the goal of understanding what intelligence is. Therefore, AI is a highly interdisciplinary field of science including engi-neering, philosophy, mathematics and logics, psychology and other natural sciences. The high potential for controversies in such an interdisciplinary field of study becomes already obvious by the fact that there is no common definition of what intelligence is (Boden, 1981). Is intelligence something that goes beyond the natural materialistic world and is "human-exclusive"? Or can it be reached by technical reproduction of the human brain and its cognition?

One more and more frequently discussed problem that lies in such questions and even in the term "artificial intelligence" itself is the issue of anthropomorphizing AI. This often leads to a wrong perception of AI for laymen as well as for researchers and professionals resulting in ethical and epistemological problems (Salles, Evers, & Farisco, 2020). The term "artificial intelligence" can be traced back to John Mc Cathy who used it as the name for a conference in Dartmouth (Pallay, 2020) instead of talking of cybernetics – which was the more frequently used term for self-regulatory systems (Zimmerli & Wolf, 1994). Since intelligence is perceived as something intrinsically human by most people, the tendency to anthropomorphize in the field of AI can already be found at this very beginning of the discipline.

But even before the term "artificial intelligence" was used for the discipline, Alan Turing published a seminal work on the question "can machines think?" which can be seen as one of the most influential works since the beginning of AI, predicting several developments already years in advance (Turing, 1950; Muggleton, 2014). Nevertheless, Turing is criticized for anthropomorphizing his descriptions and possibilities of intelligent machines (Proudfoot, 1999).

In this essay the question will be discussed whether or not Alan Turing's concept of the "imitation game" enhanced and enhances the tendency for anthropomorphism in the field of AI – and if so, to what extent. Therefore, this essay will attempt to give a critical explanation of the concept of anthropomorphism in the field of AI from a historical point of view. First of all, a brief summary on general aspects of AI will be given, with a focus on the development of AI since Alan Turing's work on intelligent machinery. Afterwards a short description of the concept of anthropomorphism will be discussed, including also a psychological point of view. Based on that, examples for anthropomorphism in AI will be analyzed within the context of the previously described development of the discipline, focusing specifically on aspects and concepts in the development of AI that have led to anthropomorphisms in particular.

In this context Alan Turing's "Imitation Game" will be discussed focusing on the question whether the way the test is designed enforces the anthropomorphism in AI and what impact it had on the further development of the discipline. At the end a brief description of the pre-history of AI should give a possible explanation on which historical basis Turing describes his test and why it is possibly misinterpreted in some cases.

Therefore, in this essay the concept of anthropomorphism itself is the subject of study and not its consequences.

2 Fundamental Aspects about AI today

2.1 General

Before focusing on anthropomorphism in AI it is crucial to mention some basic aspects of the field to better understand what the state of the art is and how artificial intelligence works today. The first problem that needs to be addressed is the missing definition of what intelligence in general and artificial intelligence in particular is. Most books and AI researchers characterize AI as the science of making machines perform tasks that could previously only be carried out by human beings (Bolander, 2019; Boden 1981). When using this characterization, one should be very critical about the human-centric view on intelligence that is carried by this perspective. Russel and Norvig therefore separate the development of artificial intelligence in a human-centered part and a rational part (Russel & Norvig, 2010). It is important to mention at this point that AI is not the science of computers but rather of computer programs (Boden, 1981).

Currently AI programs are very specific and most programs are only capable of solving single tasks and tend to fail when addressing multi-dimensional problems. Nonetheless AI often outperforms humans when it comes to problems it is capable of solving (Bolander, 2019). But what kind of problems are these? This question is reduced by some AI researchers to a simple rule of thumb: the easier the problem is for humans the harder it is for AI programs to solve. More correctly this means that it needs to be possible to clearly define a problem. Therefore, human and artificial intelligence are complements at the moment (Bolander, 2019). At this point it is important to mention the concepts of strong and weak AI. Strong AI is based on the assumption that machines can have their own mind, while weak AI states that real intelligence can only be simulated by machines (Kaplan, 2017). Recent trends in AI try to focus on the development of artificial general intelligence through deep neuronal networks, a technique that imitates the basic principle of neurons and can thereby simulate a learning process that is known as machine learning (Bolander, 2019). This approach of creating AI is called the connectionist approach. Another approach that was mainly focused in the beginning of the development of AI is the symbolic or cognitive approach (Zimmerli & Wolf, 1994; Bolander, 2019). How these two approaches developed in the history of AI will be described in the following section to show which influence these different paradigms have on the anthropomorphism in AI.

2.2 Development of artificial intelligence

Zimmerli and Wolf split up the history of artificial intelligence into the discussion history and the pre-history. They regard Turing's paper on "computing machinery and intelligence" as the beginning of the philosophical discussion on AI (Zimmerli & Wolf, 1994). The development of the field since then will be described in this part of the essay. As previously mentioned, the field of AI can be split up into two basic paradigms: cognitivism or symbolic AI and connectionism or sub-symbolic AI. In his paper Turing himself already described the different possible development directions on how AI could be achieved. Even though the basis for the connectionist paradigm was already laid very early in the development of AI with the Hebbian Theory and the Rosenblatt Perceptron, research was focused on the symbolic paradigm in the beginning (Zimmerli & Wolf, 1994). As mentioned before the beginning of the AI era was introduced with the Dartmouth conference. At this beginning stage the research was focused on learning about cognitive processes and using the processing methods of digital computers to make assumptions on what human thinking is and how it works (Zimmerli & Wolf, 1994). The basic assumption of this approach is that thinking is the manipulation of symbols. Therefore, complex patterns of thought and action can be reduced to simple mechanisms. Following from that the method of this paradigm is rather top-down, developing static programs out of observed cognitive rules that can be used to solve different problems. One of the most important approaches of this time was pursued by Newell and Simon who developed the general problem solver. For the development of the program, peoples problem solving strategies were observed and formalized with the goal of finding general patterns that could be used to solve different tasks with one program (Zimmerli & Wolf, 1994). Based on that work Newell and Simon formulate the physical symbol system hypothesis: "a physical symbol system has the necessary and sufficient means for general intelligent actions [...] by 'general intelligent action' we wish to indicate the same scope of intelligence as we see in human action" (Newel & Simon, 1976). This means that symbol manipulation is the necessary basis for all kinds of intelligent thinking and as a result thereof machines can reach human-level intelligence because the symbol system is a sufficient means to reach intelligence (Pallay, 2020).

But further developments of the general problem solver push against the limits of this approach because it was not possible to show that the program was really capable of solving different problems (Zimmerli & Wolf, 1994).

That is why in the 1980s a paradigm shift from the symbolic to the connectionist paradigm took place. The Rosenblatt perceptron whose development stagnated since the 1960s was further developed and multi-layer neuronal networks became the preferred way of programming AI. The novelty of this approach compared to the symbolic approach is that the algorithms allow machine learning based on statistics and reinforcement (Zimmerli & Wolf, 1994; Russel & Norvig, 2010).

Both paradigms were foreseen by Alan Turing who in the last chapter of his paper on "computing machinery and intelligence" describes different strategies on achieving learning machines: through programming which is rather top-down and can be compared to the symbolic approach and through a learning child machine which can be assigned to the connectionist paradigm (Turing, 1950; Muggleton, 2014).

By analyzing the historical development of AI, we can see the principle assumptions on which it is based. This makes it clearer to understand why anthropomorphism has always accompanied the research field and how it is deeply connected to its structure of thinking.

2.3 Symbolic and connectionist paradigm

In this chapter the present state of the differences between connectionism and the symbolic approach will be outlined in more detail. Bolander describes the difference as follows. Connectionism is the mimicking of neuronal processes (for example neurons) and symbolic AI follows an abstract model of human problem solving. This top-down approach should simulate the highest level of human cognition and has the advantage of predictability and explainability while it is generally delimited to single problem solving with low flexibility. Connectionist AI is based on machine learning from experience. This learning is not 100% predictable because it is based on statistics. As both approaches complement each other in their weaknesses and strengths current AI research is searching for a coupled approach (Bolander, 2019). This third probability of a coupled approach

5

to create artificial intelligence was also already proposed by Alan Turing with a program using logic, probabilities and learning (Muggleton, 2014).

It becomes clear that even fifty years ago Alan Turing's ideas had a big influence on the development paths of AI (Muggleton, 2014). But does this also apply to the discipline's tendency towards anthropomorphism? To further analyze this question the next chapter will present how anthropomorphism is used in AI research and give some theoretical explanations on why it is used.

3 Anthropomorphism in Artificial Intelligence

3.1 A brief psychological theory on anthropomorphism

According to the oxford dictionary anthropomorphism is "the practice of treating gods, animals or objects as if they had human qualitites" (Oxford, 2020). In an article on anthropomorphism by Epley the likelihood of anthropomorphism is traced back to three different psychological determinants: (1) the accessibility and applicability of anthropocentric knowledge, (2) the motivation to understand and explain the behavior of other agents and (3) the desire for social contact and affiliation (Epley, Waytz, & Cacioppo, 2007). All three determinants can possibly be seen within the field of AI especially in the public sector. This is a result of intended anthropomorphism but also of poor scientific communication (Salles, Evers, & Farisco, 2020). The essay will focus on the professional's and AI researcher's tendency to use anthropomorphisms, since this is where the structural embeddedness of this tendency lies and is partly reflected by public actors. In the case of developers and researchers the tendency to anthropomorphize can be traced back to the psychological determinant of the motivation to understand and explain behavior (Salles, Evers, & Farisco, 2020).

3.2 The use and possible reasons for anthropomorphism in Artificial Intelligence

Already Alan Turing used several anthropomorphisms in his paper on "computing machinery and intelligence" which will be described in more detail later (Proudfoot, 1999; Proudfoot, 2011). Anthropomorphism in AI can have different shapes: the intentional attribution of typical human traits like consciousness; the attribution of expressive behavior like smiling; or thinking that AI follows human-like ways of functioning (Salles,

6

Evers, & Farisco, 2020). Especially the last point will be examined more extensively in the following part because it can be assumed that it is the basis for the other two points. The assumption that AI works in a human-like way can be traced back to the historical development of the discipline as shown before and increases the risk of attributing human traits to AI technologies. This can at least be seen in the new hype of human-level AI (AI that has the same capabilities as humans) (Proudfoot 2011).

These tendencies can mainly be assigned to the human-centered approaches for AI that were described by Russel and Norvig. Human-centered AI systems are successful when they can generate human-like performances. In their book Russel and Norvig ascribe the Turing Test to the human-centered approaches (Russel & Norvig, 2010). These approaches are especially susceptible to anthropomorphisms because they are partly based on empirical observations of human behavior (Russel & Norvig, 2010; Salles, Evers, & Farisco, 2020). The general problem solver of Newell and Simon is a typical example for such human-centered thinking and shows that the anthropomorphism used in AI research lies not only in the communication of the researchers but also in the understanding of its functioning. The physical system symbol hypothesis reduces human thinking to the manipulation of symbols and therefore justifies that AI can reach human-level intelligence. This focus on reproducing the human intelligence and also the assumption that it is possible for computer programs to do that, is already at the core of setting human and artificial intelligence as equal and comparing them.

But also in the connectionist paradigm which does not try to reproduce human cognition with a top down approach but by a bottom up learning process, anthropomorphism is already embedded in the understanding of its basic functioning by comparing it to neuronal networks which are derived from the functioning of the human brain (Salles, Evers, & Farisco, 2020). This is done without artificial neuronal networks having a lot to do with real neurons (Ullmann, 2019). As a result of this anthropomorphic rhetoric crucial differences between these systems and the functioning of human thinking are often overseen. These differences were also discussed by Watson who mentions three major distinctions: (1) the brittleness of deep neuronal networks, which means that the learned behavior of the system breaks down, facing only little changes in the data, (2) the inefficiency of deep neuronal networks because large amounts of data and large training sets are needed whereas humans can often generalize out of a low amount of data (one shot learning) and (3) the myopia of deep neuronal networks failing to recognize the interrelationship between data (for example seeing a face even though the eye and the mouth are interchanged) (Watson, 2019).

These examples and their analysis show that the anthropomorphism in both paradigms of AI – connectionist and symbolic – originates from the interpretation that AI can work in a human-like manner and therefore reach human level competences. To show what another, non-human-centered interpretation of AI looks like that is less susceptible to anthropomorphisms, the concept of mindless intelligence by Jordan Pollack will be briefly introduced.

3.3 Beyond human mind

Jordan Pollack criticizes the human-centered orientation of AI research in his paper on "mindless intelligence" from 2006. He states that one of the disciplines biggest mistakes is to see human level-intelligence as the greatest existing intelligence (Pollack, 2006). Other authors also support this argument by stating that intelligence is not the privilege of chosen ones (Bovenschulte & Stubbe, 2019).

Pollack states that by trying to simulate symbolic consciousness, human intelligence – and notably one part in particular: the human mind – cannot be reproduced (Pollack, 2006). As described previously he also traces this back to the beginning of AI as a discipline which strongly believed that the human intelligence and the human mind can be simulated by symbol manipulation and therefore not by focusing on other aspects of intelligence. One striking argument against this opinion is John Searles "Chinese room" which is a thought experiment that showed, that symbolic manipulation doesn't create an understanding or consciousness of the processed symbols (Searle, 1980). Pollack uses this argument to show that the "symbolic mind is a myth" (Pollack, 2006, p. 3).

Still Pollack also claims that the connectionist approach follows the pattern to model human cognition. Therefore, he calls for mindless intelligence which in his view is "intelligent behavior ascribed to any process lacking a mind-brain" (Pollack, 2006, p. 3). "Algorithms shouldn't be anthropomorphized and don't need any cognitive accoutrements. Such processes could be complex natural systems that appear intelligent but lack a cognitive apparatus " (Pollack, 2006, p. 4). He calls these systems "ectomental" and gives several examples where such "ectomental" processes appear (evolution itself, embryo development, the immune system or the GAIA hypothesis) (Pollack, 2006). The paper ends with the following sentence: "symbolic mind is a self-aggrandized fiction told to make sense of a few pounds of mindlessly intelligent meat" (Pollack, 2006, p. 7). This can be underlined by a quote from Serebriakoff: "intelligence always strives for its own perfection" (in Bovenschulte & Stubbe, 2019). With his critique on the development of AI Pollack shows that by trying to reproduce human thinking, AI research was locking itself into an imagination that strongly promoted anthropomorphism in the field.

4 Interim Conclusion

Since the beginning of AI as a scientific discipline anthropomorphism was not only part of its rhetoric but also part of its basic understanding. According to the human-centered approach the main goal of AI was always to reach human-level AI either by simulating cognitive processes or imitating neuronal structures. That's why the algorithms them-selves were anthropomorphized. AI was rarely thought independently from the human mind. On the one hand this limitation lead to an increasingly anthropomorphic rhetoric about AI topics and on the other hand to a limited development of the discipline itself. Pollack calls for a new orientation of the discipline that does not focus on human-intel-ligence and symbol manipulation but starts to concentrate on other intelligent proce-dures because AI can only reach its full potential when algorithms are not anthropomor-phized anymore (Pollack, 2006). Still the open question to be answered is why AI devel-oped in such a human-centered way? Alan Turing is seen as the father of AI, being able to foresee many of its developments before the term was even coined (Muggleton, 2014). Turing's large influence raises the question whether his work pushed the disci-pline into the human-centered, anthropomorphizing direction that it has taken on from its beginning until know? Turing himself used numerous anthropomorphism that will be discussed in the following chapter. By describing the "imitation game" he also gave a kind of definition outlining at what point a machine can be seen as an intelligent entity. The following part of the essay will analyze Turing's work to find out whether or not it contributed to anthropomorphizing the discipline in the following years.

5 Turing and anthropomorphism

5.1 The "imitation game"

First of all, to discuss Turing's influence on the anthropomorphism in artificial intelligence it is necessary to give a brief description of the "imitation game". Turing developed this thought experiment by trying to give an answer to the question whether machines can think. Therefore, he describes a game where an interrogator alternatively asks questions to a hidden computer and a hidden human. The communication is reduced to simple text messages. The interrogator needs to find out which of the respondents is the machine. The machine itself has the goal to answer the questions in such a way that the interrogator is deceived and cannot identify it. As a result, Turing develops a new question to answer the old question: "can machines think?":

"Is it true that by modifying this computer [C] to have an adequate storage, suitably increasing its speed of action, and providing it with an appropriate programme, C can be made to play satisfactorily the part of A in the imitation game, the part of B being taken by a man?" (Turing, 1950, p. 8).

Turing states that answering the question "can machines think?" is irrelevant. By replacing the question with the previously mentioned one he distances himself from giving any definition of what thinking is and how machine thinking could look like. Therefore, he raises the question: "May not machines carry out something which ought to be described as thinking but which is very different from what a man does?" (Turing, 1950, p. 2f.). He considers the question, whether or not a machine can think sufficiently answered when a machine can imitate human behavior.

5.2 Anthropomorphism used by Turing

One of Turing's predictions is, that the usage of language within the society will change in a way that anthropomorphic descriptions of machines will be generally used and accepted (Turing, 1950). At this point it is interesting to mention that Turing himself already uses a couple of anthropomorphisms in his paper that should be described in this chapter. The main anthropomorphisms can be found in his last chapter: "learning machines" (Proudfoot 1999; Proudfoot 2011). There he describes possible ways of how machines can be created that will succeed in the imitation game. Amongst others he mentions the possibility of a "child machine" that could be educated. This machine, Turing states, "could not [be] send […] to school without the other children making excessive fun of it" (Turing, 1950, p. 20). He continues by supposing to use the behavioral technique of punishment and reward to teach the machine (Turing, 1950).

Moreover the "imitation game" could intentionally be interpreted to compare humans and machines directly in the way it is designed. The question if this is really anthropomorphizing machines should be discussed in the following chapter.

5.3   Discussion of the Turing Test

As described in Stuart's and Russel's book on artificial intelligence, Turing's thoughts can be ascribed to a human-centered approach because the intelligent machines he describes should be capable of imitating human behavior (Russel & Norvig, 2010). The questions that needs to be asked now is, whether this approach of Turing is already anthropomorphizing AI because the imitation of human behavior is interpreted as intelligent behavior of the machine?

To give an answer to this question that is based on Turing's paper is difficult because Turing himself doesn't give a clear definition of what thinking is. He even distances himself from searching for an answer on the question "can machines think?" because he regards this question as too trivial to be answered (Turing, 1950). Moreover, he states that the thinking process of a machine can strongly deviate from what humans are doing. During his discussion of possible objections against machine intelligence he also discusses the problem of consciousness. But instead of giving reasons why it is possible that machines could have a kind of consciousness he rather states that "instead of arguing continually over this point, it is usual to have the polite convention that everyone thinks" (Turing, 1950, p. 11).

By operationalizing the question whether machines can think through the construction of the imitation game instead of giving a clear answer on what machine thinking could look like, Turing bypasses to ascribe human attributes to AI.

Turing does not specify weather strong AI or only weak AI will be possible but rather dissolves the differences between both terms (without the concepts already existing at this time) (Russel & Norvig, 2010). In the sense of Pollack, Turing was not suggesting that intelligent machines need to have a mind (even though he discusses the possibility with the question if a machine can be "supercritical" and the "skin-of-an-onion" analogy) (Turing, 1950, p. 18f.).

Turing gives another important hint on the differences between humans and machines when he describes the universality of digital computers. He states that electricity is not a similarity characteristic of digital computers because they can also be mechanical like the calculation machine of Babbage from the 19th century. At this point he highlights the difference to the human nervous system which is based on electrical as well as chemical processes. He disproves the comparison between nerval systems and digital computers because digital computers rely on mathematical functional analogies (Turing, 1950).

Some interpretations of the imitation game even show that it prevents the anthropomorphic description of machines to some extent. Proudfoot states that the design of the imitation game does avoid the forensic problems of anthropomorphism (Proudfoot, 2011). She attributes this to two aspects of the design of the imitation game: it provides (1) a disincentive to anthropomorphize in favor of the machine because the likelihood to lose the game by not identifying the machine is increased when the interrogator is anthropomorphizing the computer and (2) a control to screen for anthropomorphic bias in favor of the machine because the tendency of the interrogator to anthropomorphize is independent from the real identity of the respondents and does therefore not favor the machine. By this, Proudfoot concludes that the test design is mitigating anthropomorphism (Proudfoot, 2011).

6   Pre-History of AI

Before coming to the final conclusion this chapter should take up some important aspects of the pre-history of AI because it can give relevant hints about why anthropomorphisms in AI are so commonly used and also helps to put some of Turing's work into a context that supports us to better understand it.

In the end the anthropomorphism in AI also depends on the question to what extend human thinking is and was seen as a reproduceable process that can be possibly transferred on other structures than the brain. The basis for this was already made hundreds of years before the term AI was even coined. According to Zimmerli and Wolf the foundation of AI is the connection of formalization, calculation and mechanization (Zimmerli & Wolf, 1994). Hobbes was connecting the syllogistic of Aristoteles with mathematical

constructs and therefore saw thinking as a mathematical construct that can be calcu-
lated (Russel & Norvig, 2010). Also, Descartes was supporting the hypothesis that a uni-
versal mathematic (methesis universalis) exists, by which all processes can be explained.
Nonetheless Descartes was a proponent of dualism, seeing mind as something sepa-
rated from the material world (Russel & Norvig, 2010).

Based on this, from a materialist point of view the reproduction of human thinking was
only a matter of technical and mathematical development.

However, Gödel was proving the limitations of this thinking by his incompleteness the-
orem, showing that every formal system has statements that could neither be proved
nor disproved (Russel & Norvig, 2010).

Still based on this history the symbolic logic became the method of choice for the reproduction of human thinking (Pallay, 2020). A lot of today's assumptions in AI are based
on the materialistic pre-assumption that human thinking is rationalizable and that the
mind can therefore be reproduced because the brain is subject to natural law (Proudfoot, 1999). Based on that it is attractive to ascribe human attributes like consciousness
or a free will to AI because if humans have these attributes AI must also be capable of
having it. Or seeing it the other way around, if machines can't have consciousness this
also applies to humans (Kaplan, 2017). This view already opens the gate for anthropomorphism in AI.

But are these assumptions supported by Turing's imitation game? Not directly because
as previously described Turing doesn't give an answer to the mind-body problem and
the imitation game doesn't test for cognition but just for the imitation of human behavior.

7   Conclusion

The essay was analyzing the pre-history and discussion history of AI with regards to the
tendency of anthropomorphisms in the discipline. As Alan Turing's work had and still has
an enormous influence on the field special focus was put on his paper on "computing
machinery and intelligence".

As one result of the analysis it can be summarized that anthropomorphism in AI is not
only a problem of rhetoric and communication but also an issue of its fundamental understanding to focus on the reproduction of human mind which has its origin already in

13

the pre-history of AI. This tendency was criticized by Pollack who is asking to focus on mindless artificial intelligence rather than anthropomorphizing algorithms by trying to reproduce the symbolic mind (Pollack, 2006).

To what extend Alan Turing's work was pushing this development in AI is difficult to say. Some authors see Turing as part of the human-centered approach which can be interpreted as reinforcing the anthropomorphism in AI (Russel & Norvig, 2010; Salles, Evers, & Farisco, 2020). Other authors regard Turing's test as misunderstood and propose new interpretations on how the test could even inhibit anthropomorphism (Proudfoot, 2011). Since Pollack criticizes the focus on the reproduction of human mind in AI as a reason for anthropomorphized algorithms, it is also important to analyze what Turing's perspective on the mind-body problem was. By distancing himself from the question "can machines think" and bringing up the imitation game Turing was also distancing from giving an answer to the question if machines can or should have a mind or if their way of thinking could be totally different to the human way of thinking. By replacing the question "can machines think" with the question described in chapter 5.1, he is already avoiding any form of anthropomorphizing the functioning of AI because he excludes the term "thinking".

Even though Turing was using anthropomorphism by himself he was not anthropomorphizing the functioning of possible intelligent machines. The tendency of anthropomorphizing the basic functioning of AI rather has its origin in the symbolic approach. This has large implications on the ethical and philosophical discussion but also the social perception of AI which themselves need to be analyzed in more detail.

Bibliography

Boden, M. A. (1981). *Artificial Intelligence and natural man.* Brighton: Harvester.

Bolander, T. (2019). *Proceedings of Pragmatic Constructivism, 9*(1), 17-24.

Bovenschulte, M., & Stubbe, J. (2019). Einleitung: "Intelligenz ist nicht das Privileg von Auserwählten". In V. Wittpahl, *Künstliche Intelligenz - Technologie | Anwendung | Gesellschaft* (Bd. 1). Heidelberg: Springer Vieweg.

Epley, N., Waytz, A., & Cacioppo, J. T. (2007). On seeing human: A three-factor theory of anthropomorphism. *Psychological Review, 114*(4), 864-886.

Kaplan, J. (2017). Philosophie der künstlichen Intelligenz. In J. Kaplan, *Künstliche Intelligenz: Eine Einführung* (Bd. 1, S. 81-103). Frechen: mitp Professional.

Muggleton, S. (2014). Alan Turing and the development of Artificial Intelligence. *AI Communications, 27*, 3-10.

Newel, A., & Simon, H. A. (1976). Computer Science as Empirical Inquiry: Symbols and Search. *Communication of the ACM, 19*(3), 113-126.

Oxford. (12. 08 2020). *Oxford Learner's Dictionary*. Von https://www.oxfordlearnersdictionaries.com/definition/english/anthropomorphism?q=Anthropomorphism abgerufen

Pallay, C. (2020). Vom Turing-Test zum General Problem Solver. Die Pionierjahre der künstlichen Intelligenz. In K. Mainzer, *Philosophisches Handbuch Künstliche Intelligenz*. München: Springer Fachmedien Wiesbaden GmbH.

Pollack, J. B. (2 2006). Mindless Intelligence. *IEEE Intelligent Systems, 21*, 50-56.
Proudfoot, D. (21. 01 2011). Anthropomorphism and AI: Turing's much misunderstood imitation game. *Artificial Intelligence, 175*, 950-957.

Proudfoot, D. (30. 4 1999). How Human Can They Get. *Science, 284*, 745.

Russel, S., & Norvig, P. (2010). *Artificial Intelligence - A modern approach* (Bd. 3). New Jersey: Pearson Education Inc.

Salles, A., Evers, K., & Farisco, M. (31. 05 2020). Anthropomorphism in AI. *AJOB Neuroscience, 11:2*, 88-95.

Searle, J. R. (1980). Minds, Brains and Programs. *Behavioral and Brain Science, 3*, 417-457.

Turing, A. (1. 10 1950). Computing Machinery and Intelligence. *Mind, 49*(236), 433-460.

Ullmann, S. (15. 2 2019). Using neurosciecne to develop artificial intelligence. *Science, 363*(6428), 692-693.

Watson, D. (2019). The rhetoric and reality of anthropomorphism in artificial intelligence. *Minds and machines, 29*, 417-440.

Zimmerli, W. C., & Wolf, S. (1994). *Künstliche Intelligenz: Philosophische Probleme.* Stuttagrt: Reclam.